Original title:
Nighttime Wishes, Morning Dreams

Copyright © 2024 Creative Arts Management OÜ
All rights reserved.

Author: Tobias Sterling
ISBN HARDBACK: 978-9916-90-694-1
ISBN PAPERBACK: 978-9916-90-695-8

Glimmers of the Golden Hour

The sun dips low, a soft embrace,
Its tender light begins to chase.
Shadows dance on fields of green,
In this magic, peace is seen.

Whispers of gold in the evening's breath,
Nature sings of life and death.
Birds in flight, a fleeting sight,
Chasing dreams in fading light.

Moments blend, the day grows old,
Stories in hues of orange and gold.
Time stands still, a gentle pause,
In this beauty, hearts just cause.

As twilight beckons, stars break free,
In the glow of dusk, we find glee.
The world slows down, a whispered vow,
Glimmers shine in the golden hour.

Dawn's Awakening

The sun peeks over hills, so bright,
A canvas painted with golden light.
Birds begin their morning song,
Nature stirs where dreams belong.

Soft whispers dance upon the breeze,
Awakening flowers, swaying trees.
Night's quiet linger fades away,
Embracing life in a brand new day.

Shadows of Hopes at Midnight

In the stillness, shadows creep,
Whispers of dreams buried deep.
Stars above, a guiding song,
Holding wishes, hopes so strong.

Through the darkness, light may flow,
Revealing paths we do not know.
In the quiet, hearts take flight,
Finding solace in the night.

Celestial Yearnings

Beneath the moon's soft silver gaze,
We dream of worlds lost in a haze.
Wishing on stars that twinkle bright,
Yearning for peace, and endless light.

Galaxies dance in silent space,
Each moment pure, a warm embrace.
In cosmic tales, our hopes reside,
As we wander, hearts open wide.

The Light Before Daybreak

A shimmer hints at dawn's embrace,
Night whispers goodbye, a gentle grace.
Stars fade softly into the blue,
As shadows dance, bidding adieu.

The horizon blushes with the sun,
A new day whispers, 'You have won.'
In this moment, dreams take flight,
As we welcome the morning light.

Echoes of Forgotten Wishes

In the garden where shadows dance,
Whispers linger, a silent chance.
Dreams once bright, now fading light,
Lost in time, out of sight.

Beneath the stars, hopes softly call,
Memories rise, then gently fall.
Fragments of joy, woven with care,
Echoes of dreams released in air.

Serene Visions of Dusk

As daylight fades, the world grows still,
Soft hues paint the sky, a tranquil thrill.
Whispers of night bring comfort and peace,
In the quiet, all worries cease.

Dreams awaken in the twilight's embrace,
Gentle stars twinkle, a celestial grace.
Each moment savored, time feels slow,
In serene visions, our spirits glow.

A Glimmer in the Darkness

In shadows deep, where hope feels thin,
A flicker stirs, inviting us in.
Through the veil of night, a light shines bright,
Guiding lost hearts towards what is right.

In the quiet hush, resilience grows,
Emerging strength from trials and woes.
With each heartbeat, courage will spark,
A glimmer found within the dark.

Sunlit Aspirations

Golden rays break through the dawn,
Whispering dreams that carry on.
Hope takes flight on the wings of day,
Chasing the clouds, come what may.

Through fields of gold, our visions soar,
Each aspiration opens a door.
In the warmth of light, we find our way,
Sunlit paths where our hearts can play.

Enchanted Echoes in the Twilight

Whispers dance in evening light,
Breezes carry dreams in flight.
Stars awaken, softly gleam,
Painting night with silver dream.

In the hush where shadows play,
Magic lingers, night and day.
Heartbeats blend in twilight's kiss,
Moments lost in gentle bliss.

Moonlit paths entwine our fates,
Underneath the starlit gates.
Every echo, every sigh,
Holds the secrets of the sky.

As the night begins to fade,
Memories in depths are laid.
Enchanted echoes softly call,
Binding spirits, one and all.

The Serene Bridge Between Worlds

Between the realms where silence sings,
A bridge of dreams, on silver wings.
Time stands still, as shadows part,
Uniting every drifting heart.

Gentle whispers flow like streams,
Carrying our deepest dreams.
With every step, our spirits roam,
Finding peace in twilight's home.

In this space, our fears dissolve,
A world where mysteries evolve.
Embracing dusk, we come alive,
On this bridge, we learn to thrive.

Together, hand in gentle hand,
In unity, together stand.
The threads of fate begin to weave,
In this realm, we truly believe.

Flickers of Light in Hidden Dreams

In the corners of my mind,
Flickers of light I hope to find.
Whispers of stories yet untold,
In hidden dreams, the brave and bold.

With every spark, a chance to fly,
Through the shadows, we'll defy.
Into realms where visions bloom,
Chasing echoes beyond the gloom.

Softly glimmering, the night inspires,
Igniting deep, forgotten fires.
Through the darkness, we will steer,
Finding treasures hidden near.

These fleeting lights will guide our way,
Through the night to break of day.
In every flicker, we will trust,
Awakening the dreams we must.

Reveries of Shadows and Gleams

In the dance of light and shade,
Silent dreams are gently laid.
Whispers linger in the night,
Hopes ignite with soft delight.

Reveries so sweetly spun,
Stories told once day is done.
With every shadow, secrets weave,
In the gleam, we learn to believe.

Treading paths where echoes lay,
In the dark, we find our way.
Every heartbeat, every sigh,
Links the earth to endless sky.

In this realm where dreams take flight,
Shadows bend to greet the light.
Hold my hand as whispers call,
With every gleam, we rise and fall.

Echoes of the Moonlight

Soft whispers call from the darkened skies,
Gentle beams dance where the stillness lies.
A silver glow on the whispering stream,
Where shadows waltz in a dreamy theme.

Clouds drift slowly, a fleeting embrace,
Kissing the night with a tranquil grace.
Stars like jewels, they shimmer and gleam,
Igniting the depths of the midnight dream.

Dawn's Tender Promises

The horizon blushes with golden hue,
Birds start to sing, as the day breaks through.
Whispers of sunlight caress the land,
Awakening blooms with a loving hand.

Softly, the world shakes off its night,
Promises linger in morning light.
With every ray, hope takes its flight,
Painting new dreams in skies so bright.

Nocturnal Reveries

In the quiet heart of the midnight hour,
Dreams unravel like a blooming flower.
Chasing stardust through the velvety dark,
Each whispered secret ignites a spark.

Shadows play where the night winds roam,
Cozy and warm, in the dark we comb.
Mysteries hide in the silvery glow,
Among the whispers of tales we know.

Dreams Wrapped in Twilight

As daylight bids its soft adieu,
Night unfolds in a cloak of blue.
Stars emerge, twinkling above,
Wrapping the world in a shroud of love.

Time slows down, in this gentle embrace,
Every heartbeat finds its rightful place.
With twilight's kiss, the spirits play,
Dancing in dreams till the break of day.

Dreams that Dance with the Dawn's Breeze

In the hush of morning light,
Dreams take flight, a soft delight.
Whispers of hope on gentle air,
Carried away without a care.

Colors burst with vibrant hue,
Painting skies of deepest blue.
Every breeze a tender sigh,
As dreams and dawn begin to fly.

The Quiet Migration of Stars

Across the night, they softly glide,
Stars in silence, worlds collide.
Flickering points of distant tales,
Carried forth on cosmic gales.

In their dance, a timeless grace,
Guiding wanderers through space.
Every twinkle, a wish to share,
A journey whispered in the air.

Whispers of a Starlit Sky

In velvet depths, the silence hums,
While secrets spun in stardust come.
Each glimmer holds a story sweet,
As night's embrace begins to greet.

Low whispers weave through moonlit beams,
Echoing softly within our dreams.
Stars align, a fleeting tune,
Singing softly to the moon.

Slumber's Gentle Embrace

In the cradle of the night,
Dreams wrap tight in soft twilight.
Resting under a blanket deep,
Where lullabies and shadows seep.

Time slows down, the world is still,
Captured in a tranquil thrill.
Slumber calls with tender grace,
In her arms, we find our place.

Moonbeam Reflections

Soft whispers dance on silver beams,
Casting dreams in twilight seams.
The world below, serene and bright,
Beneath the watchful, glowing light.

Ripples glide on a midnight lake,
Each ripple formed a silent wake.
In the stillness, shadows play,
As moonbeams chase the night away.

The Inhabitant of the Night

In the silence, a figure roams,
Bathed in shadows, far from homes.
Eyes like stars, they pierce the dark,
Carving paths where dreams embark.

Whispers of the night unfold,
Tales of secrets yet untold.
With each breath, a mystery grows,
Underneath the moonlit throes.

Where the Stars Belong

High above in the velvet sky,
Stars converge, they laugh, they sigh.
In their glow, stories ignite,
Guiding souls through the night.

Across the vast, eternal sea,
A tapestry of dreams are free.
Where destinies intertwine and weave,
In the cosmos, we believe.

Twilit Prophecies

In the twilight, shadows linger,
Softly creased by fate's own finger.
Every whisper holds a sign,
Promises drawn in the cosmic line.

As day departs, the night unveils,
Mystic visions on gentle trails.
Guided by the stars' embrace,
The night reveals its timeless grace.

Stirring Whispers of Awakening

In the soft dawn's light, whispers flow,
Awakening dreams in the morning glow.
Gentle breezes kiss the trees,
Nature hums sweet melodies with ease.

Birds take flight, tracing arcs in the sky,
As the world stirs, with a hopeful sigh.
Flowers bloom, painting colors anew,
In each petal, a story's cue.

The sun ascends, a radiant crown,
Chasing away the shadows down.
Every heartbeat syncs with the day,
In the freshness, old fears decay.

Embrace the light as it softly streams,
Filling our hearts with tender dreams.
We rise with the sun, renewed and free,
In the whispers of morning, we find our key.

Ethereal Dreams at Dusk

As twilight descends, the sky ignites,
A canvas painted with shades of night.
Stars awaken, twinkling so bright,
In ethereal dreams, we take flight.

Whispers of shadows, secrets untold,
In the cool of the evening, feelings unfold.
The horizon blurs, boundaries erase,
In the twilight glow, we find our place.

Moonbeams dance on the shimmering lake,
In the stillness of dusk, every heart aches.
For the magic that lingers in the air,
An enchanting embrace, beyond compare.

Time slows as the world holds its breath,
In the balance of twilight, life and death.
Our spirits soar in this fleeting trance,
In ethereal dreams, we find our chance.

Celestial Murmurs at Daybreak

When the night surrenders to morning's grace,
Celestial murmurs fill every space.
The first light kisses the sleeping hills,
Awakening the world with tender thrills.

Gentle hues brush the sky's face,
As the day unfurls, a soft embrace.
Clouds dance lightly, a pastel parade,
In the breath of dawn, our worries fade.

In the chorus of nature, life begins,
Each note a promise that gently spins.
With every heartbeat, hope takes flight,
In celestial whispers, we find our light.

Boundless skies stretch, a canvas wide,
As day emerges, we cast aside.
With the dawn, we dream and dare,
In the morning's hush, love fills the air.

The Alchemy of Dusk and Dawn

In the tender embrace of dusk and dawn,
Alchemy brews, as shadows are drawn.
Mysteries linger in twilight's wake,
In the stillness, new beginnings take.

Colors collide in a dreamy haze,
As night intertwines with the sun's rays.
Moments suspended, time stands still,
In this alchemy, we find our will.

The veil between worlds grows thin and frail,
Echoes of magic in the nightingale.
As stars fade away and the sun appears,
A dance of transitions, the heart cheered.

In the mingling of light where secrets reside,
Awakened spirits, a journey untried.
We explore the thresholds, bold and drawn,
In the alchemy of dusk and dawn.

A Sojourn into the Unknown

In shadows deep, I take my step,
A path unwrought, where silence wept.
The stars above, they guide my way,
Into the night, I choose to stay.

The whispers call, a haunting tune,
Beneath the watchful, silver moon.
Each twist and turn, a dance of fate,
In mysteries held, I contemplate.

Through valleys dark, by rivers wide,
I journey forth, with dreams as guide.
A heart that yearns, a spirit bold,
In every step, new stories told.

With every breath, a world unknown,
To find my place, to find my own.
In echoing night, I roam alone,
A sojourn vast, where seeds are sown.

Whispers of the Dawn Chorus

The first light breaks, the colors bloom,
Nature stirs, dispelling gloom.
A symphony of notes takes flight,
In soft embrace of morning light.

The gentle chirps, a warm delight,
Speak of hope, as day turns bright.
Each feathered voice, a tale to share,
In harmony, they fill the air.

From branches high, to fields below,
They sing of joy, they weave and flow.
In every tune, the earth awakes,
A bond so pure, in silence breaks.

With every note, a promise made,
In whispers soft, our fears do fade.
As dawn unfolds its golden hues,
The chorus sings, to greet the muse.

Songs of Solace

In quiet nights, when dreams collide,
Tender tunes, my heart's true guide.
They wrap around, like warm embrace,
In melodies, I find my place.

A voice so soft, it mends the seams,
In every chord, I weave my dreams.
Each note a balm, for weary souls,
In songs of love, our spirit rolls.

Through whispers low, and laughter bright,
We share our tales beneath the night.
In simple strums, we find our way,
In solace found, we choose to stay.

The music flows, a river wide,
In every beat, our hearts reside.
A timeless dance, a sacred space,
In songs of solace, we embrace.

Mystical Auras

In twilight shades, the colors blend,
A spectral dance, where dreams transcend.
The mystic glow, a guiding light,
Illuminates the depths of night.

From realms unseen, the whispers call,
A tapestry woven, a cosmic thrall.
With open hearts, we seek to see,
The magic held in you and me.

Each wandering soul, a story told,
In vibrant hues, the world unfolds.
In every flash, a spark divine,
In mystical auras, we align.

As stardust swirls in evening's grace,
The universe hums, a warm embrace.
Together we shine, with love entwined,
In mystical auras, forever blind.

Songs in the Silence

Whispers of winds in the night,
Catch the soft glow of the light.
Echoes dance in shadowed space,
Melodies drift with gentle grace.

Stars hum tunes, a cosmic choir,
Breath of the cosmos, whispers higher.
In the stillness, secrets awake,
Notes of dreams in silence stake.

A Glance Towards Tomorrow

Fingers trace the line of fate,
Each moment held, we contemplate.
Future glimmers, bright and clear,
Hope arises, drawing near.

Horizons stretch, the sun will rise,
Painting colors in the skies.
With each dawn, a chance to grow,
A heartbeat whispers, 'Let it flow.'

Dreaming in the Indigo

In a sea of deep indigo,
Thoughts afloat, like stars aglow.
Visions dance in twilight's embrace,
Painting worlds, time and space.

A canvas vast, where dreams take flight,
In the depths of tranquil night.
Close your eyes, let stories spin,
Journey forth, let life begin.

Tapestries of the Cosmos

Threads of light weave through the dark,
Creating patterns, a vibrant arc.
Galaxies swirl, a grand ballet,
In cosmic hues, night turns to day.

Each star a stitch, each planet a seam,
Crafting the fabric of every dream.
Infinite wonders, vast and wide,
In the tapestry, we all abide.

Slumbering in Celestial Embrace

In the hush of night's soft sighs,
Stars twinkle like whispered dreams.
Wrapped in clouds, the silence lies,
Beneath the moon's gentle beams.

A lullaby in cool night air,
Worlds collide in quiet grace.
Sweetest peace hangs everywhere,
Time slows in this sacred space.

Drifting thoughts on breeze take flight,
Cradled in night's tender arms.
Each heartbeat a starry light,
Woven into night's soft charms.

Within this slumber, heart finds rest,
In celestial embrace anew.
Whispers of love, softly pressed,
In dreams, the heart's wings pursue.

A Moonbeam's Gentle Yearning

A moonbeam spills on silver streams,
Casting shadows that softly dance.
In the quiet, the heart dreams,
Of a love ignited by chance.

Waves in rhythm, whispers sweet,
Kisses of night on skin so pale.
Stars align with each tender beat,
Painting the tale of a ship's sail.

Through the twilight, wishes soar,
Guided by the moon's soft glow.
Yearning hearts forevermore,
In the embrace of stars, they flow.

Hopeful sighs on winds take wing,
In the night, each secret shared.
Love, a song the nightbirds sing,
Under the sky, souls ensnared.

Transitions of Twilight Tides

Shadows stretch as day does fade,
Twilight beckons, softly bright.
In this tender serenade,
The world pirouettes in light.

Ocean waves hum lullabies,
Kissing shores with gentle grace.
As the sun dips, evening sighs,
Stars emerge to take their place.

Colors blend, a soft refrain,
From gold to deep indigo.
In this dance, no hint of pain,
Just a fluid ebb and flow.

Time suspends in twilight's glow,
Each heartbeat a fleeting tide.
In this moment, dreams can grow,
As night's magic will abide.

Celestial Wishes in Silent Shadows

Celestial wishes on night's breeze,
Whispers of dreams like shadows cast.
In the dark, the heart finds ease,
Secrets held within night's grasp.

Stars twinkle with tales untold,
In quiet corners of the sky.
Each moment, a wish unfolds,
Beneath the stars, our spirits fly.

Silent shadows weave their thread,
A tapestry of heart's delights.
In the stillness, dreams are bred,
In the arms of vast starry nights.

Hopeful sighs on stardust clouds,
Cradled in the night's embrace.
Among the silent, joy enshrouds,
In the dark, our fears efface.

Night's Cradle of Hope

In the stillness of the night,
Dreams take flight beneath the stars,
Whispers weave through the dark air,
A tapestry of hope is ours.

Lullabies from the moonlight,
Softly cradle hearts aflame,
Every shadow hides a secret,
Each moment calls out a name.

Resting in the gentle glow,
Awakening a silent wish,
In the quiet, magic stirs,
As the soul begins to swish.

Hold this peace within your heart,
Let it guide you through the haze,
For in night's enchanting arms,
Hope forever gently stays.

Sunbeams on Slumbering Souls

Dawn creeps in with golden rays,
Kissing dreams that linger near,
Awakening the world anew,
With whispers only hearts can hear.

Softly dancing through the leaves,
Sunbeams warm the tranquil scene,
Every petal starts to wake,
In the light, the soul is clean.

Nature's choir sings so sweet,
Melodies that soothe the strain,
In the hush of morning light,
Joy returns to life again.

Brighter days are on the rise,
As slumbering souls greet the sun,
With each ray a promise sparks,
A new journey just begun.

The Nocturnal Reverie

Underneath the velvet sky,
Dreams unfold like silk in night,
Stars become our guiding friends,
In the darkness, time takes flight.

Gentle winds carry our thoughts,
Through the alleys of the mind,
Every shadow tells a tale,
Secrets of the night entwined.

Moonlight drapes the world in calm,
With its touch, silence prevails,
Wrapped in wonder, we wander,
Following the nighttime trails.

As slumber calls us deep within,
We dance in thoughts, so bittersweet,
In this reverie of night,
Life's mysteries we all greet.

Awakening in Shades of Dawn

With the blush of morning light,
Night's embrace begins to fade,
Colors burst upon the scene,
In the glow, new dreams are made.

Birds begin their jubilant songs,
As the world starts to arise,
Every shade paints life anew,
Inspiring hope beneath the skies.

Gentle breezes kiss the earth,
Whispers of a fresh new start,
In the garden of today,
The beauty sings within the heart.

Time awakens with the sun,
Promising a path ahead,
In each hue, we find our way,
Guided by what hope has said.

A Symphony of Light and Dark

In shadows deep where whispers play,
The light breaks through, a bright array.
Each note a pulse, a heartbeat's grace,
Together they weave, a timeless space.

The night brings forth a soothing calm,
While daylight casts its warming balm.
In harmony, they dance and twine,
A symphony of the divine.

Stars twinkle bright in endless sea,
Drawing dreams from you to me.
In the quiet, the world ignites,
A ballet of the dark and lights.

Together they sing, new tales unfold,
In silver whispers and hues of gold.
Eternal struggle, vast and stark,
The beauty lies in light and dark.

Comets and Morning Glories

Comets blaze across the night,
Chasing stars with fleeting light.
Morning glories climb and sway,
Awakening to a brand new day.

Each petal holds the sun's embrace,
While comets dash with timeless grace.
They paint the sky in vibrant hues,
Telling tales of cosmic views.

With every rise, new hopes ignite,
In the stillness of the twilight.
A dance of dreams, both wild and free,
Nature's call, a symphony.

Comets fade yet leave their trace,
Morning glories bloom in place.
In every glance, a world reborn,
Through night and day, love is sworn.

Fables of Dreams

In whispered words, the stories flow,
Fables of dreams, where wonders grow.
Each heartbeat echoes through the night,
A canvas painted with pure delight.

Characters emerge from shadows cast,
Their journeys woven through the vast.
With every chapter, hope takes flight,
In realms unseen, where dreams ignite.

A dragon flies, a maiden sings,
The magic of tales, what joy it brings.
Through every twist, a lesson learned,
In the flames of passion, the heart yearns.

So gather 'round and hear the lore,
Of dreams that knock upon the door.
In every fable, a piece of soul,
Unlocking paths to make us whole.

Dreams Sown Beneath the Sky

In fields of hope, the seeds are sown,
Beneath the sky, where dreams are known.
With gentle hands and hearts so wide,
We nurture wishes, side by side.

The winds of change weave through the air,
Carrying whispers of dreams laid bare.
Each blade of grass, a promise bright,
Of futures blooming in morning light.

Stars align in patterns rare,
Guiding us through this earthly lair.
In silent moments, our spirits soar,
Embracing dreams, forevermore.

Beneath the vast, unending sky,
Our hopes take root, our spirits fly.
Together we'll weave a world anew,
With dreams sown deep, for me and you.

Flickers of Hope

In the shadowed night, a gleam shines,
A whisper of dreams in fragile lines.
Every spark dances, bright and true,
In the heart's chamber, hope breaks through.

Silken threads weave through the dark,
Kindling warmth, igniting a spark.
Where despair looms, light finds its place,
A tender smile, a soft embrace.

In the silence, a heartbeat's chime,
Threads of solace, woven through time.
Beneath the weight of endless skies,
Hope's gentle flicker never dies.

So let the stars guide the way ahead,
With every step, let courage spread.
For even in shadows, dreams will cope,
In every moment, flickers of hope.

Luminosity in Lullabies

Soft whispers drift on a silver night,
Carried by moonbeams, pure and bright.
In lullabies, a world we find,
Wrapped in dreams, the heart unwinds.

Gentle echoes of love's embrace,
Illuminate the silent space.
With every note, fears fade away,
As shadows dance, and night turns to day.

Twinkling stars weave celestial tunes,
Under the gaze of wandering moons.
In every sigh, a promise rests,
The soul awakened, it gently flrests.

Hold close the warmth of every line,
In tranquil rhythms, hearts align.
For in the stillness, magic thrives,
In luminous lullabies, life survives.

Fragments of Celestial Tales

In the cosmos where dreams unfold,
Whispers of stories are softly told.
Galaxies spin in an endless dance,
Each star a hope, a fleeting chance.

Fragments of light in the velvet sky,
Crystals of time that drift and fly.
With every twinkle, wishes ascend,
Binding the past and future, blend.

Echoes of ancients, spirits set free,
Charting the path for you and me.
In the night's embrace, our hearts ignite,
Filling the void with sparks of light.

So gather the fragments, weave them tight,
In the tapestry of the endless night.
For every tale that the heavens share,
A piece of magic dances in the air.

The Embrace of Dusk

When the sun dips low and shadows play,
The sky is painted in hues of gray.
Night unfurls its velvet cloak,
In this hush, the heart awoke.

Crickets sing in the cooling breeze,
Rustling leaves whisper ancient trees.
In the twilight, memories bloom,
Casting soft light in the gathering gloom.

With every stroke of the night's brush,
Time slows down, and pulses hush.
Moonlight drapes like a tender sigh,
As the day fades, and stars comply.

In the embrace of dusk, we find our peace,
A moment's grace that grants release.
For in the melding of night and day,
Hope gently rises, lighting the way.

The Anthem of the Dawn

Awake, the sun reveals its grace,
Whispers of light in every space.
Birds sing sweetly in the trees,
A symphony carried by the breeze.

Gold spills over the waking land,
Promises painted by nature's hand.
Hope rises with the morning's glow,
As the world shakes off the night's woe.

A gentle warmth upon the skin,
New beginnings, where dreams begin.
With every heartbeat, life renews,
In the dawn's embrace, the heart pursues.

Together, we greet the day anew,
The anthem of dawn, bright and true.
In every moment, a chance to soar,
The sun bids us live, explore, and more.

Moonlit Musings

Under the veil of night so deep,
The moon casts dreams for hearts to keep.
Whispers of silver in the dark,
Guiding thoughts like a quiet spark.

Stars adorn the celestial dome,
Each one a story, a distant home.
In tranquil silence, shadows play,
As visions dance and softly sway.

The night is alive with endless sighs,
Echoes of secrets and lullabies.
In this stillness, our spirits rise,
Finding peace under endless skies.

Moonlit musings weave their spell,
In the heart's chamber, they softly dwell.
A tapestry of dreams unfurled,
We wander gently through the world.

Lullabies to the Stars

Close your eyes and drift away,
To a realm where wishes sway.
Stars above sing soft and clear,
Lullabies for you to hear.

In the quiet of the night,
Dreams take wing and take to flight.
Galaxies hum of hope and peace,
In their embrace, all worries cease.

Cradle your heart in starlit grace,
Feel the warmth of love's embrace.
As cosmic whispers fill the air,
You are cherished, you are rare.

Lullabies to the stars so bright,
Guide you through the velvet night.
In dreams, we'll dance among the beams,
Together, woven into seams.

A Canvas of Shadows

In twilight's glow, the shadows play,
Forming whispers of dusk's ballet.
Each outline tells a tale untold,
On a canvas of night, mysteries unfold.

Colors blend in the fading light,
Creating worlds, both strange and bright.
The dance of darkness, a wistful sight,
Enigmas painted, left to invite.

Echoes linger in the cool night air,
Stories beckon, waiting to share.
Hushed tones of the evening sky,
In the silence, dreams softly lie.

A canvas of shadows, rich and deep,
Holding secrets that the night will keep.
With every breath, the heart will roam,
In shadows, we find our way back home.

Portraits of Sleep

Whispers weave through moonlit night,
Silent sighs in gentle flight,
In shadows deep, the dreams take form,
The heart finds peace, a soothing warm.

Fleeting visions dance and glide,
In the corners where hopes abide,
Each thought a brush, a stroke of grace,
In stillness found, a sacred space.

Lost in moments, drifting far,
Chasing tales where wonders are,
With lids that close, the world slips slow,
As sleep weaves tales, a soft tableau.

Through velvet clouds, the spirit flies,
In realms where all the magic lies,
Embrace the night, its sweet refrain,
In portraits bright, we meet again.

Beneath a Blanket of Dreams

Stars twinkle soft in a cooler sky,
Beneath the blanket, we softly sigh,
Each thread a story, a wish made true,
In slumber's hold, we find what's new.

Crickets sing their lullabies,
While fireflies weave through quiet skies,
In this cocoon, time holds its breath,
Wrapped in joy, we dance with rest.

Moonbeams touch our peaceful face,
Gentle whispers of night's embrace,
Dreams unfold like petals wide,
In every heart, our hopes reside.

As dawn approaches, shadows flee,
In morning light, we're wild and free,
Yet still, we cherish night's sweet theme,
Forever held beneath the dream.

In Search of Sunlit Shores

Waves caress the sandy land,
Footprints trace a journey planned,
In golden rays, we seek the light,
Where shadows fade, and hopes ignite.

Seagulls call to skies so blue,
In harmony, the soul feels new,
With every heartbeat, we explore,
The vast expanse of sunlit shores.

Palm trees sway and breezes play,
Time retreats, it slips away,
In each splash, a dream unfurls,
Life awakens, as joy swirls.

Beneath the sun, we find our song,
In moments where we all belong,
Together on this sandy floor,
We dance the dance of ocean's roar.

The Dream Weaver's Palette

A painter's touch with colors bright,
With gentle strokes, she weaves the night,
Each dream a hue, a tale to tell,
In whispered notes, we fall under her spell.

From twilight's grasp to morning's glow,
Visions blend, a vibrant show,
With every shade, emotions flow,
A canvas rich, a world to sow.

In the depths of slumber's art,
Imagination plays its part,
A tapestry of desires spun,
Each thread a memory, every one.

As dawn arrives, the colors fade,
Yet in our hearts, the dreams cascade,
The dream weaver's palette remains in view,
A treasure chest of hopes anew.

Secrets Beneath the Moon

Whispers linger in the air,
As shadows play beneath the trees.
The moon reveals a hidden lair,
Where secrets drift upon the breeze.

Veils of night cloak every thought,
In silken shades of mystery.
The stars, a tapestry, are wrought,
With tales of dreams and history.

Flickering lights twinkle above,
Each glimmer holds a story true.
An echo of forgotten love,
Beneath the moon's soft silver hue.

In silence, all the worlds collide,
As night unfolds its gentle song.
In shadows where the secrets hide,
The heart knows it has belonged.

Pathways of Dawn

At dawn, the world begins to stir,
With gentle light that breaks the night.
Each path emerges, line blurred,
In hues that blend from dark to bright.

The sun ascends, a golden guide,
Over hills and valleys wide.
With every step, new joys abide,
As warmth replaces where we bide.

Birdsongs weave through the morning air,
A symphony of hope reborn.
Through fields refreshed with dew so rare,
Life awakens with each new morn.

Embrace the journey, hold it tight,
For every dawn brings tales to share.
With open heart and mind in flight,
We find the beauty waiting there.

The Dance of the Horizon

A dance begins where sky meets land,
With colors blending, bright and bold.
The horizon stretches out at hand,
A canvas rich with tales untold.

Clouds twirl gracefully in the skies,
As shades of purple, gold, and blue.
With every glance, the spirit flies,
To where the sun bids night adieu.

Mountains bow as shadows fall,
While whispers of the winds arise.
In silent grace, the beauty calls,
As day surrenders to starry skies.

Together, they weave a refrain,
Of nature's song, both wild and free.
In harmony, they break the chain,
Inviting us to simply be.

Awakened in the Twilight

As daylight fades, the shadows grow,
A hush envelops all around.
In twilight's glow, our spirits flow,
Where mysteries and dreams abound.

The moon peers down, a watchful eye,
With secrets nestled in its light.
In gentle whispers, we comply,
And dance along the edge of night.

Stars paint the sky with twinkling grace,
Guiding hearts through the unseen.
In stillness, we embrace this space,
A moment caught in shades of green.

Awakened souls, we weave and blend,
In twilight's arms, we find our peace.
As shadows play and night descends,
Our spirits soar, our fears release.

The Sway of Sleep's Soft Serenade

In the quiet night so deep,
Whispers call from dreams to keep.
Gentle tides of peace and light,
Rock me softly into night.

Moonlit shadows dance and sway,
Cradled softly, here I lay.
Stars become my lullaby,
In their glow, my spirits fly.

A symphony of sighs and stars,
Dissolves the weight of worldly scars.
Each note a touch, a sweet embrace,
In sleep's arms, I find my place.

Wrapped in warmth of velvety sleep,
I surrender, deeply, steep.
As dreams unravel, softly spun,
In this sway, our hearts are one.

Embraces Under a Starry Veil

Beneath the sky, our hearts entwined,
Among the stars, our souls aligned.
Each twinkle tells a tale of grace,
In this moment, time we trace.

The night wraps us in tender light,
A blanket soft, a sweet delight.
With every sigh, the world eclipses,
Lost in love, the heart elicits.

Whispers dance on evening's breeze,
As shadows weave between the trees.
In the glow of silvery beams,
We'll sail away on starlit dreams.

Your hand in mine, a cosmic plan,
Underneath this vast, grand span.
In this embrace, no fears remain,
Forever bound in love's refrain.

Awakening to the Symphony of Light

With dawn's first blush, the world awakes,
As golden rays break night's keepsakes.
Nature stirs with every hue,
A symphony of life renews.

Birds trill softly from the trees,
Their melody rides on the breeze.
The sun climbs high, a radiant cue,
Each beam a promise, fresh and true.

In the warmth, new dreams ignite,
Casting shadows from the night.
Every heartbeat plays a part,
In this concert of the heart.

Step by step, the day unfolds,
With tales of courage, bravery told.
Awake to life, let worries cease,
In the light, find your peace.

The Lure of the Midnight Canvas

Night paints the sky with strokes of dark,
Each star a dream, a glimmered spark.
On this canvas, secrets draw,
Whispers linger, beauty's law.

The moon, a ghostly silver muse,
Guides lost souls who wander, choose.
Each shadow holds a tale untold,
In midnight's grasp, the heart grows bold.

Colors blend and shadows shift,
In every curve, a hidden gift.
The night invites a dance of grace,
Where every heartbeat finds its place.

Brush the starlight, taste the night,
In this allure, the soul takes flight.
On the canvas where dreams collide,
Embrace the lure, let hearts abide.

Stardust and Daylight

In the quiet of twilight's embrace,
Whispers of stardust softly trace.
The dawn awakens, a gentle sigh,
Daylight spills through a painted sky.

Moments dance like fireflies bright,
In the tapestry woven by night.
With every heartbeat, dreams take flight,
Under the warmth of morning light.

Nature stirs in a golden glow,
Life unfolds in a vibrant flow.
Stardust mingles with open skies,
Daylight glistens where beauty lies.

The cycle of night to day divine,
A reminder of life's sweet design.
Holding the magic of the unseen,
In stardust and daylight, we glean.

Midnight's Gratitude

Beneath the quilt of midnight's hue,
Stars are whispers of dreams come true.
Gratitude blooms in the stillness deep,
Where secrets of the universe sleep.

The moon, a guardian so wise,
Watches over with silvered eyes.
Each heartbeat echoes a silent prayer,
For moments cherished beyond compare.

Soft shadows linger, time's gentle touch,
Reminds us always, we've been through much.
In darkness, we find the strength to rise,
With midnight's grace, we build our skies.

In solitude, love's comfort gleams,
Awakening the heart to seal our dreams.
Under the stars, gratitude flows free,
A dance with the night, just you and me.

The Transition of Hope

At the brink of dawn's first ray,
Hope ignites in the light of day.
Transition whispers through the trees,
In every rustle, a gentle breeze.

The night departs, casting shadows long,
In the quiet, we find our song.
With each heartbeat, we feel the lift,
The promise of change, a precious gift.

Clouds drift softly, painting the sky,
Carrying dreams on wings that fly.
In the space where light meets shade,
Hope blooms brightly, never to fade.

Embrace the dawn, the heart's true call,
With every struggle, we stand tall.
In the transition, we find our way,
Guided by hope, come what may.

Hues of the Unseen

In shadows cast by the setting sun,
The hues of the unseen slowly run.
Colors emerge like whispers unheard,
Nature's palette, a vibrant word.

A symphony plays in silence sweet,
Life's hidden shades where colors meet.
Every moment, a brushstroke fine,
In the canvas of time, hearts intertwine.

Through the veil where dreams reside,
The unseen dances, a graceful slide.
Each hue speaks tales of love and grace,
Painting our souls in this sacred space.

Awake to the wonders of what we miss,
In every blink, a fleeting kiss.
The unseen colors our world anew,
In the magic of moments, life's true hue.

Silhouettes of Desire

In twilight's glow we linger near,
Whispers soft, a secret clear.
Shadows dance as hearts ignite,
In the hush of the velvet night.

Dreams entwined like silken thread,
Bound by hope, where love is spread.
Fingers touch, a fleeting spark,
Illuminates the hidden dark.

Longing paints the air with grace,
In every glance, a warm embrace.
Time stands still, the world a blur,
With every heartbeat, feelings stir.

Beneath the stars, our spirits fly,
In the night's embrace, we soar high.
Silhouettes of what could be,
In this moment, you and me.

Between the Stars and Sun

A canvas stretched from dusk to dawn,
Colors blend, as night moves on.
Horizon whispers tales untold,
In this realm, the brave and bold.

Celestial bodies light the skies,
While daylight fades, and twilight sighs.
Between the stars, our dreams take flight,
Chasing shadows into the night.

The sun dips low, a golden hue,
Bathing all in warmth so true.
Yet in the dark, a spark remains,
A promise held through joy and pains.

In this space where time suspends,
Moments merge, where love transcends.
Between the stars, our hearts align,
In the dance of fate, you are mine.

Soft Shadows of Tomorrow

In the dawn's embrace we stand,
Future bright, with gentle hand.
Hopes are born in the morning light,
Guiding us through day and night.

Promises whispered by the breeze,
Like soft shadows, they aim to please.
Dreams awakening from deep slumber,
Counting moments, with a number.

Each step forward, a choice we make,
Woven paths, through love we break.
In the tapestry of life we sew,
The soft shadows of tomorrow grow.

With every heartbeat, a new refrain,
Chasing joy, through pleasure and pain.
Guided by love, we shall find our way,
In soft shadows, come what may.

Glimmers of Mirth

In laughter's wake, we find our light,
Glimmers of joy, so pure and bright.
Moments caught in fleeting glee,
Echoes of happiness, wild and free.

Bubbling laughter fills the air,
Sweet memories take us everywhere.
With every smile, a story shared,
In cherished moments, we are bared.

Twinkling eyes beneath the moon,
In gentle nights, our hearts attune.
Glimmers of mirth in every glance,
A dance of souls in life's romance.

Together we weave the fabric of fun,
As life unfurls, we become one.
In this tapestry of joy we weave,
Glimmers of mirth, we believe.

Whispers of the Starlit Sky

In the night where dreams reside,
Softly glimmers, stars collide.
Whispers echo, tales untold,
Secrets of the night unfold.

Moonbeams dance on silver streams,
Guiding lost and wandering dreams.
In the stillness, hearts align,
Underneath the vast divine.

The cosmos sings a gentle tune,
Beneath the watchful eye of moon.
Celestial kisses linger long,
In this space, we all belong.

A tapestry of light above,
Weaving threads of hope and love.
With every star, a wish takes flight,
In the whispers of the night.

The Dawn's Secret Promises

When the first light starts to bloom,
Casting off the night's dark gloom.
Gentle rays begin to glow,
In their warmth, the world will flow.

Birds awaken, sing anew,
A melody that feels so true.
With each note, the heart expands,
As the dawn's embrace commands.

Mist like whispers fades away,
Every moment holds its sway.
Secrets wrapped in golden hues,
A canvas painted in soft blues.

Promises of a brand new start,
Breathe life into the eager heart.
With open arms, the world shall greet,
The dawn's magic, pure and sweet.

Serenade of the Moonlit Heart

Underneath the silver light,
Hearts unite in quiet night.
A serenade of softest sighs,
Promises beneath the skies.

Shadows dance on whispered dreams,
In the glow, love gently beams.
Every glance, a spark ignites,
In the hush of starry nights.

The moon, a witness to our fate,
Guides our souls through love's estate.
With each heartbeat, time suspends,
In this world where magic blends.

Together here, we find our song,
In a space where we belong.
A serenade, soft as a sigh,
Underneath the endless sky.

Dreams Woven in Twilight

As the day begins to fade,
Twilight casts a gentle shade.
Secrets linger in the air,
Echoes of a silent prayer.

Stars emerge, the night unfolds,
Carving dreams like tales of old.
In this moment, still and bright,
Wish upon the coming night.

Time slows down, the world ignites,
In the glow of fading lights.
Wisps of magic drift around,
In this sacred space, we're found.

Woven dreams, like threads of gold,
Stories waiting to be told.
In twilight's grasp, our hearts shall soar,
To realms unknown, forevermore.

A Journey through Stardust

In the quiet of the night, we sail,
Through currents of light that never pale.
Each star a whisper, a tale untold,
A path of silver, a shimmer of gold.

Galaxies swirl in a cosmic dance,
We follow the trails, entranced by chance.
With every heartbeat, the universe sings,
A tapestry woven with celestial strings.

Nebulas bloom like petals of fire,
Igniting our dreams, lifting us higher.
We wander through shadows, embrace the glow,
In this infinite sea, we let our hearts flow.

As the dawn breaks, we gather the light,
Carrying stardust, our souls take flight.
In the echo of cosmos, we find our place,
A journey of wonder, a timeless embrace.

Beyond the Horizon

Where sky kisses sea, the colors collide,
A canvas of dreams where hope does abide.
We chase the sun as it dips low,
Unraveling secrets the tides softly know.

The whispers of waves tell stories anew,
Of travelers bold and the journeys they drew.
Each step on the shore, a promise to keep,
Of adventures that flourish, and memories deep.

In twilight's embrace, shadows extend,
Our hearts intertwine, as lovers and friends.
With every curve of the coast, we explore,
Unlocking the beauty of what lies in store.

As stars ignite in the velvet sky,
We gaze in wonder, let out a sigh.
For beyond the horizons, where dreams are spun,
A world of sweet magic awaits everyone.

Unseen Gardens of the Night

In the hush of darkness, blooms softly shake,
Whispers of petals, like dreams they wake.
Moonlight dapples the leaves with grace,
In gardens unseen, we lose ourselves in space.

The nightingale sings of love long past,
Notes weaving stories that flutter and last.
In shadows we wander, hand in hand,
In the magic of night, together we stand.

Secretive flowers, with fragrances rare,
Invite the midnight to linger and care.
Each breath a secret, each heartbeat a theme,
In this hidden garden, we dwell in a dream.

As dawn approaches, the stars start to fade,
The beauty of night in our hearts is laid.
Through unseen gardens, forever we roam,
In the arms of the night, we find our way home.

The Breath of Awakening

In the stillness of morn, when the world holds its breath,
Nature awakens, defying the death.
A chorus of colors splashes the sky,
As whispers of dawn weave a soft lullaby.

The dewdrops shimmer, like jewels on the grass,
Each moment a treasure, too precious to pass.
With the first rays of light, the shadows retreat,
Reviving the life that was lost in the heat.

Birds flutter gently, heralding day,
Their melodies soar, chasing silence away.
In the warmth of the sun, we stretch and we grow,
In the breath of awakening, life starts to flow.

As the world comes alive, we dance with delight,
Embracing the gift of this wonderful light.
In the cycle of seasons, we find our own song,
In each breath of the morning, we learn to belong.

The Veil of Cosmic Yearning

Stars whisper secrets, distant and bright,
Dreams drift in silence, lost in the night.
Galaxies beckon with shimmering light,
Hope floats like lanterns, ready for flight.

Wishing on comets, we reach for the sky,
Veils of the cosmos, where lost spirits lie.
Each heartbeat echoes, a celestial sigh,
In the vastness of space, where wonders reside.

The moon, a guide with her tender embrace,
Navigates wanderers through boundless space.
With every heartbeat, we long for that place,
Where love intertwines with the stars' gentle grace.

We dance with the shadows, the dark and the wide,
In timeless devotion, our dreams we confide.
The veil of our yearning becomes our guide,
As we trace the cosmos, with hope and with pride.

Glistening in the Gloom

Crimson leaves flutter, kissed by the breeze,
Whispers of autumn, a dance through the trees.
Moonlight cascades in a silvery stream,
Shadows awaken, igniting the dream.

Stars peek from corners where darkness resides,
Glistening softly where mystery hides.
In the heart of the night, the world seems to change,
Embracing the beauty, both tender and strange.

Glimmers of starlight bathe all in delight,
Painting the shadows with jewels of the night.
Hope stirs beneath as the moon takes her throne,
Glistening whispers weaved from the unknown.

In gloom, we discover a spark of our soul,
Pieces of magic that help us feel whole.
As night wraps its arms, we find our own tune,
In the depths of darkness, we glisten, we bloom.

Night's Embrace

The sun dips below, the shadows grow long,
Night whispers softly, a soothing song.
Stars ignite softly, like candles in air,
Wrapping the world in a blanket so rare.

With every heartbeat, the stillness unfolds,
Secrets unravel as the night's story molds.
Dreams mingle gently like dew on the grass,
In night's gentle cradle, we let moments pass.

The moon, a guardian, watches us dream,
Guiding our hearts down the silvered stream.
Night's embrace cradles, finds solace in dark,
A sanctuary woven, where hope leaves its mark.

We linger in echoes, where shadows take flight,
Finding ourselves in the depths of the night.
Each sigh is a promise, each whisper a chance,
In night's sweetest solace, our spirits will dance.

Day's Promise

Morning light spills like a golden sweet song,
Awakening dreams that have lingered too long.
Birds serenade softly, a chorus so near,
Painting the dawn with a palette of cheer.

Colors emerge as the night fades away,
Each moment reborn in the light of the day.
Hope dances lightly on beams from above,
Whispers of promise wrapped up in pure love.

Trees stretch their branches, reaching for sky,
In every leaf rustle, they sigh and they fly.
The world opens wide, like a warmhearted hug,
Embracing the beauty, the warmth, and the tug.

As sun peaks its head, at the dawn's gentle chime,
We gather our dreams in the river of time.
Day's promise delivered with each new sunrise,
Reminding our spirits to ever arise.

The Carpet of Nightfall

As twilight descends, stars begin their dance,
The carpet of nightfall invites us to chance.
Velvet skies whisper, secrets of old,
Tales of the ancients in glimmers unfold.

Through shadows we wander, tracing the light,
Awash in a tapestry woven by night.
Each thread is a dream, each color a sigh,
In the quiet embrace where the lost wishes lie.

The moon casts her glow, a serene silver guide,
Carrying whispers where mysteries bide.
Nocturnal melodies wrap round like a shroud,
In the depths of the quiet, our souls feel so proud.

So rest in the night, on this carpet so fine,
Let dreams be your compass, let starlight align.
In the heart of the dark, where possibilities bloom,
The carpet of nightfall unfolds every room.

The Call of the Nocturne

When night wraps the world in a soft embrace,
Whispers of shadows begin to dance.
The moon spills secrets, a silvery trace,
Inviting the dreams of a mystic romance.

Stars wink brightly in the velvet sky,
Each a story of hope and despair.
The call of the nocturne lures hearts to fly,
To places where magic drifts softly in air.

In the hush of the dark, echoes are spun,
Melodies twinkle like dew on the grass.
Awakening spirits, we join the fun,
To take flight with the night, let the moments pass.

As dawn gently teases the dark to retreat,
The echoes of night meld with morning's song.
The call of the nocturne, though bittersweet,
Lingers forever, where dreams now belong.

Luminous Echoes

In deep of the night, where silence reigns,
Luminous echoes softly appear.
Whispers of light through the dark remain,
Filling the void with hope and cheer.

Each flicker a tale of a moment lost,
Bound in the threads of shimmering time.
Through shadows they scatter, no love is tossed,
Connecting our souls, a celestial rhyme.

The dance of the light, a guiding friend,
Charting the path where we long to go.
These echoes from stars that will never end,
Illuminate hearts in the twilight's glow.

So raise your eyes high, let your spirit soar,
Embrace the luminous whispers that call.
In each flicker, find what you're yearning for,
A promise of love that unites us all.

Reflections in the Quiet

In the shadows' embrace, softness resides,
Reflections awaken in night's gentle hand.
Quietly waiting, where stillness abides,
The heart finds its rhythm, a delicate strand.

Whispers of thoughts drift through the air,
Like leaves caught in breezes, they twirl and fly.
In moments of stillness, we learn how to care,
The silence speaks truths that we often deny.

Stars gleam above like eyes full of wisdom,
Inviting our sorrows to drift far away.
In quiet reflections, we find a kingdom,
Where dreams intermingle, unbroken, they stay.

So pause in the night, take a breath, and feel,
The echoes of peace that invite us to stay.
In reflections of quiet, our wounds begin heal,
As shadows embrace what the heart longs to say.

The Bridge Between Stars

Across the vast seas of shimmering night,
Lies a bridge forged in whispers and light.
Connecting the dreams that soar through the space,
Uniting the hearts of a common grace.

Step lightly upon the ethereal beams,
Where wishes entwine with the fabric of fate.
Each footfall a promise, a journey of dreams,
A tapestry woven, yet never too late.

In the dance of the cosmos, our souls intertwine,
Bound by the stardust that colors the dark.
Together we'll wander where mysteries shine,
As one with the universe, igniting the spark.

So let us walk on, hand in hand as we soar,
Across this bright bridge, eternal and free.
For we are the wishes, forever to explore,
The magic that binds you, the stars, and me.

Echoes of Dusk's Embrace

The sun dips low, a fading spark,
Whispers dance in shadows dark.
Crickets sing their evening song,
In twilight's arms, we all belong.

Leaves rustle softly, secrets shared,
As day retires, our dreams are aired.
Horizon blushes, a canvas wide,
In dusk's embrace, we take our ride.

Stars begin their nightly glow,
Casting light on paths we know.
With every breath, the world feels still,
In echoes of night, our hearts fulfill.

Hope lingers, wrapped in twilight's thread,
As evening whispers, gently spread.
In the stillness, life unfolds,
Through echoes of dusk, our story molds.

Lullabies Beneath the Stars

In the quiet of the night,
Stars emerge, a twinkling sight.
Gentle breezes hum a tune,
Lullabies beneath the moon.

Cradled by the cosmic glow,
Dreams take flight, soft and slow.
Each star a wish that finds its voice,
In the silence, we rejoice.

Baby's breath in tender slumber,
Nature whispers, soft as thunder.
Crickets play their nighttime show,
Underneath the starry glow.

With every twinkle, hopes arise,
Painting dreams in midnight skies.
Together, wrapped in night's embrace,
Lullabies in time and space.

The First Light's Gentle Caress

Morning whispers through the trees,
Sunlight dances with the breeze.
Awakening the world anew,
In golden hues, the day breaks through.

Birds start singing, sweet and clear,
Nature's symphony draws near.
Each flower opens, stretching wide,
With the dawn, our dreams collide.

The sky ignites with shades of grace,
As light spills forth, a warm embrace.
Hope unfurls in every ray,
The first light's touch begins the day.

With every heartbeat, life takes flight,
In the hush of morning light.
Together, we greet the quest,
In the dawn's gentle caress.

Visions from the Velvet Dark

In velvet dark, where dreams reside,
Whispers echo, let them guide.
Stars above weave tales untold,
In the night's embrace, we behold.

Mysteries wrapped in shadows deep,
A world awakens from its sleep.
Each flicker of light dances bold,
In visions from the dark, we hold.

The moon's soft light, a watchful eye,
Bathes the earth with silver sighs.
In this quiet, hearts can soar,
With every secret night has in store.

Let imagination take its flight,
Through worlds spun in the cloak of night.
In velvet dark, our spirits embark,
Chasing visions that leave their mark.

Milton Keynes UK
Ingram Content Group UK Ltd.
UKHW021629011224
451755UK00010B/525